Broken Silence

Ashley Vargas

BookLeaf Publishing

Presentation by *BookLeaf Publishing*

Web: www.bookleafpub.com

E-mail: info@bookleafpub.com

ISBN: 9789357210997

First edition 2022

DEDICATION

For those still finding their voice in the silence.
I hear you.

ACKNOWLEDGEMENT

My mother has taught me many things throughout my life but one lesson has shaped me into the woman I am today. From the beginning of memory, she has always told me, “Never let anyone silence you.” This simple yet powerful phrase is the reason this book exists.

Thank you Mom for always encouraging me to be honest & brave. You are the strongest woman I have ever met & I am so proud to be your daughter. I love you.

4:53 a.m.

Honesty hour
I'm afraid of all the things I do not know
Thousands of mental calculations
Still too many variables
To know which way to go
I do the best I can with the information given
But I am nothing more than a guesswork specialist
A living hypothesis
Faking confidence
I search for meaning in the night sky
Counting stars
My favorite lullaby
Mind in overdrive
No sleep

Who has the time?

Ever-Changing

Human interaction is complicated
Internal battles
Strained friendships
Reaching for connection
Watching it disappear
Distance
Palpable change
Resistance
Chess game conversations
Reading between every line
Telling stories in silence

Do we ever really know who people are?
Do we ever really meet them or just that day's representative?

They say change is the only constant
In a universe that is always evolving into the next moment
How can we hold on to the people we love,
When they too
Are ever-changing?

I'm grateful for memories.

Almost

You ask me to jump over the Moon for you & I
do
Or at least try to
But when I fall short you disregard the distance
I free-fall in the space between the Moon & your
expectations

But I am no shooting star.

59 days

It's been 59 days since you last laid on what use
to be your side of the bed
I can almost hear your breath in the silence
Still feel the contours of your body & the way
you use to wrap your arms around me
It's funny how yesterday can feel like right now
& an eternity away

So funny, but time is the only one laughing.

Dissonance

It be the mornings
Silent & motionless
Just me & these dusty memories
I open my eyes
Stretch to the sky hoping I'll somehow reach you
But where are you?
Partner turned passerby
Man turned ghost
Is this a home or a Mausoleum?
Me & this fucking photographic memory
I see you
On the walls, at the table, on the stairs, on the bed
The very air in this place reeks of you
All I can do is breathe it in
All I can do is cry it out
My lungs Struggle
Useless against the clambering of my heart
Searching for harmony
Finding only Dissonance
What happened to the music promised to me?
Songs of love
Songs of family

Instead
You left me with a broken silence
Like a record spinning endlessly
Lonely static

On repeat.

Opposite

The opposite of love is not hate
It's indifference
Seeing someone hurting
Turning a blind eye & going about your business
Asking someone how they feel & not waiting for the answer
It's unread text messages
Blocked phone calls
Reaching for someone & feeling nothing but air
It's loneliness
Looking for that spark
In someone's eye when they look at you
& realizing it's no longer there
Tarnished rings long forgotten in old jewelry boxes
Broken promises with no explanation
Like seeing the most beautiful rainbow
Fade into nothingness
The darkness of nonexistence
A void without feeling

The opposite of love is death.

Lavender Sky

Today
I ran away
Into a lavender sky
I made my sunset escape
From a life, I never needed a break from
Things change

I drove until the mountains burned behind their black outline
Like amethyst turned citrine
The yearning desire to find my own Emerald City
They say it exists
Somewhere over the rainbow
Said it's worth all the storms it took me to get here
So let this highway be my yellow brick road
Throw those red shoes in the desert
I don't want to go home
I want something better
My mother reminds me,
"The grass is not always greener
Be wise with your decisions dear daughter"

Today

I ran away
Into the lavender sky
I made my sunset escape
From a life, I never needed a break from
Things change

I drove into the darkness
passed two County lines
Smiling like I knew where I was going
Hand surfing in the wind
Music blaring
Smoke twirling
For a moment things felt easy
Singing,

"Ease on down, ease on down the road
Come on, ease on down
Ease on down the road
Don't you carry nothing
That might be a load
Come on, ease on down
Ease on down the road"

Laughing
Then a heavy silence
As I remembered
This life is everything but easy
Fear set in
Dorothy turned cowardly lion

Coyotes, jackrabbits & flying monkeys

I was not in Vegas anymore.

Trying

I’ve been trying to write a poem about yesterday
About late-night conversations under a Smokey
moon
A sky full of stars & being mesmerized
By the swing back into each other's lives
This metronome love
Beautiful until it isn’t
Dissonance
We smash our life into pieces
addicted to the crash
I’ve been trying to write a poem about yesterday
About forgiveness
After 3rd or 4th chances
Hoping the Moon can cleanse away all our sins
The present eclipsing the past
I look at you and ask,
“Can we really begin again?”
I’ve been trying to write a poem about you & me
Who we could be without yesterday’s suffering.

Magician

At that exact moment
I allow you to tiptoe back into my heart
You choose to disappear again
I keep forgetting how talented a magician you are
& me, the naive assistant
Still letting you cut me in half
Trapped in the illusion

Smiling.

Me according to you

Go ahead, ask me what's wrong
So I can try to speak & have you interrupt me
Tell me what you didn't do
All the things I'm overreacting to
Please,
Just disregard my feelings silence my truth
Go ahead, ask me to speak
So I can hear you belittle me
Just tell me how to feel, baby
Aren't I woman?
Shouldn't I be used to the weight of your
overbearing patriarchy
Continuously trying to speak for me?
Your ego
Your privilege
The noose around my neck
Choking
My silent words burning inside of me
Aren't I insignificant, baby?
Aren't I pretty?
Not enough to matter just enough for eye candy
Arm trophy
Crying but smiling
Got to put on a good show

So everyone can see your brand new shinning property
Ain't that right, baby?
Maybe
I should just lay on my back quietly
Let you impregnate me
Then get up, barefoot, cook, clean
Take care of you & the baby
Ain't that who a good little Latina is supposed to be?
Right, baby?
I mean,
These are the lessons my father tried to teach me
Beating my mother into invisibility
Screaming,

"Bitch, you think you're free?
This must be a comedy
Running your mouth like I gave you permission to
Let me remind you
You only speak when spoken to
You better learn your place, girl"

The essence of my father
Hidden behind a different face.
Go ahead, just tell me how I should feel
After all
You know me better than I do

Right, baby?

No words

No words to say
Just endless thoughts
Insomnia & familiar sounds
Screaming silence echoed down the hall
bouncing off holes in the wall
Memories lingering mid-air
Fire alarms blare
Too much smoke & mirrors
Sideshow reflections
Real or distorted perspective?
Real or illusion perfected?
Did any of it matter?
Minutes, hours, days, weeks, months & years.
I know your absence more than your presence
My favorite master musician
Play these heartstrings with precision
Just one more time
Play me something beautiful
Let me smile as you kill me

Just one more time.

Thoughts

I thought
I thought I was sure
I thought
I thought it would work
I thought
I thought I knew
I thought
I thought
I thought
I thought
I thought we had plans

& God laughed.

End

We think relationships end in massive
explosions of emotions
Thunderous clap backs & words that strike like
Lightning
Broken windows & trembling walls
But I've found that they end bit by bit
In silent conversations & unanswered cries
Blank text messages & thinking we have so
much time
They end in the silence between I love you &
I'm sorry
Buried under the weight of every word we
weren't brave enough to say
Buried in Soil rich with ego & void of sincerity
Where only shoulda, coulda & woulda bloom
A broken heart is only heard in the chest it echos
in
A deafening siren
Inescapable & unrelenting
An atomic warning only they can hear
A mushroom cloud of regret just over the
horizon
With nowhere to run
Watching their world crumble
Bit by bit

I’ve found that relationships end in ear-piercing silence.

3 Letters

The nurse walked into the room, calmly
Test results in hand, dizzy
I felt like I was floating
Not realizing I hadn't been breathing, waiting
Somewhere between twenty minutes & eternity
She sat in the same chair as before
Needles, rubber bands & plastic tubes
All used to decipher the secrets in my blood
She looked at me unblinkingly & said,
"Negative
Everything came back negative"
My eyes were filled with half relief, half despair
Knowing in that moment
He was positive
My sorrow filled the room
Like a flash flood on a dry lake bed
There was no escape
When she asked me
If I was going to continue to see him
Drowning in four years of memories
I gasped for air
I tried to answer but felt the words disintegrate
on my tongue
Letter by letter
Tiny Explosions of silence

The aftershock visible on my face
It's tremors felt only in the deepest recesses of my heart
The walls in the hospital were already shaking
& that answer shifts like tectonic plates
I couldn't handle the mental weight of my world crashing down
Don't ask me questions
Because truth is all I have to answer
She held my hand as I cried
Footsteps Intermingled with my sobbs
Then a different voice spoke to me.
A fury of medical terminology
Medications & risks
Said they have a counselor who could talk to me
"You have to understand the risks
Thoroughly
Is your life worth risking?
Don't you have a son to raise?"
The nurse repeated,
"Are you going to continue to see him?"
The room started spinning
A Mary go round out of control
Everything flying into the walls
I still wasn't breathing
"Are you going to continue to see him?"
Me drowning in this fucked up reality
"Are you going to continue to see him?"
I closed my eyes

The room disappeared & all I could see was my son
Was his life worth risking?
"Are you going to continue to see him?"
I took a deep breath & whispered

No.

Last Night

Tonight is the Last night in this house
With these memories
With these regrets
I don't know if love ever lived here
More reluctant obligation than moving in the right direction
Every scream still echos
Floorboards creak & bow from tears that never dried.

His fist print left on my son's door
A mother's day present I will for sure never forget
This house is nothing more than a mausoleum
With Two floors of skeletons hiding in closets

Lies and deceit
A smell I could never get out of the carpet
My fingers still bloody from trying to scrub
Four years of him off of my skin
This house is hell with a coat of ivory white paint
Pristine in its façade
But the darkness was always coming through the cracks

Like my smile
Sadness lingering just behind my teeth
I'm glad to leave it all behind
Although I'd rather leave it in flames
Light my blunt as people see its true nature
The roaring fire of honesty as it falls to the ground
I want to dance in its ashes & laugh
Tonight is the last night
I will sleep with ghosts & shadows of regret
May the morning come swiftly
Carry me away like a chariot of light
God's glory for the savior & his wrath in my rearview mirror

Just one more night.

Baby Mama

Baby mama
A woman I never thought I'd be
Not me
Maybe somebody else
But not A.V.
See I'm a queen
Built to create a dynasty
A wife to a king
Not A pregnant belly
With no ring
Not me
My mother raised me better
So this story cannot be
Not me
Not a thirty-something
Single mother
Not me
Not AV
Not some dude's 3rd baby mommy
Not me
I was never supposed to be the remix to my mother's story
Not me
Not the youngest of three daughters

& not my mother crying,

"Ashley
I never wanted this life for you
You were supposed to travel the world
& do all things I could never do
Not this life
not you
My baby
You're still so pretty
Just pray
God will send the right man to take care of you"

Not this story
Not me
Can't be
See I pray nightly
Been a good girl my whole life
Married right out of high school
To a man who made me his wife
But refused to make me a mother
& when he left he never said goodbye
So this was never supposed to be my life
Not me
Not Ashley
Not AV
Not book after book filled cover to cover
With teardrops & regret

Not these what-if scenarios running through my head
On the brink of madness constantly
Not me
Not the depressed girl
Spending years of her life crying

Where is my happily ever after?

Maybe they don't write those kinds of stories
About girls like me
From the hood with no daddy
Folks tell me I should be more grateful
Because my baby daddy loves his son
If I need it
He'll always break me off some money
& since my daddy wasn't around
I should know that this is a much better story
The truth is they're not wrong
I just thought
It would have been written differently
For me.

Strangers

You just keep holding on to an old version of me
It's not my responsibility to live up to a vibration
that doesn't exist anymore
& I'm sorry if you never got the apology you
were hoping for
But I'm not that girl anymore
I'm done slitting my wrists to see if I still exist
I have shit to do
To be honest I feel sorry for you
Frantically grasping for a person who's long
been gone
But I get it
The pull of what was & the knife to the gut
Every time you're reminded they're never
coming back
We all find our own way forward
You and me?
We're strangers bound together by memory
A fading picture of what used to be
An alternate reality

There is no we

There's you and there's me
New lives & an ever-changing destiny

You made your choice
Now keep that same energy.

Rain Dance

Like starcrossed lovers
Desert rain & neon lights don't dance often
But on those rare summer nights
they meet & intertwine into a dizzying monsoon of sparkle
The entire city stops to stare
Cameras flash
People gasp
Mesmerized by a sight that rivals any major marquee show
But Like most things in Las Vegas, it doesn't last long
Sometimes their love story is mear minutes
We scramble trying to get one last glimpse
Of a love We all wish was ours
Thunderclaps, a standing ovation
If you listen closely as the echo rumbles in the distance
You can hear,
"Until next time my love"
& for a moment
We can't tell the difference between the rain & our tears
On those nights
The city shines just a bit brighter

For them
And a love worth remembering.

After The Storm

My love,
This weekend was a dream of dreams
A timeless reality of you & I
A universe of we
Pleasantly diving into each other
Love cascading from our eyes like shooting stars
A wish for every kiss

My love,
We created space only we know how to fill
Pouring into the cosmic abyss of abundance
You have changed me
Pure alchemy
A heart of iron now pure gold
Hope springing from our harmony
We let the water flow
We let the love grow

My love,
I feel you inside me
Your energy healing the deepest parts.
Drop to my knees
Look at God
Fulfilling all my needs
I love you beyond all reasoning

One weekend of many

My love,
This is just the beginning.

Holy waters

I don't know much about being a hoe
I've never had a one night stand
& I was raised to be afraid of my own sexuality
So please bear with me
As I take this stage & take my stand
This poem is revolutionary
Can I talk to you about intimacy?
About making love & what divine masculinity
feels like
Pulsing the inside of me
See these legs are not open sesame
They are sentinels
Protecting my femininity
Guardians of the galaxy
Far beyond 3-D dimensionality
Which is to say
Your fuck boy shit won't work with me
You got to know how to talk to me
I'm not talking about words I'm talking about
energy
See there are levels to this pussy
I'll only fuck you if I love you
So there's no need for rubbers here
I need you to feel the God in me
& I need to feel every inch of you

Cleansed in my holy water
Sweet spirit Of unity
Let it rain
As you grip my thighs
I pull you deeper
Turn the darkness into light
You scream
I cry
We fly into the ether
Beyond space & time
I love you spoken on a whisper
Echoed through eternity
Kissing
Third eye to third eye
I see you
Hands around my neck
Demanding I surrender to you& I gladly do
Firm yet so gentle
Have you ever felt so safe
to show someone the entirety of you
This body
These scars
These wounds
This light
Take me as I am & I will show you heaven
Take you as you are & you will show me healing
Show me life
Show me breath
Breathing

I am only interested in making love
I know
In a city like this
Where Sin is king
I may be foolish
I may be lonely
But you know they say
Quality over quantity
So I will wait
As long as it takes
Touching myself in anticipation
Have you ever felt God through another person?
Divine connection
Y'all can have sex
I am only interested in heaven.

Thought I'd Be

Circling in the fog of comparison
How should my life be?
Answers hidden in life experience & envy
Haves & have nots
Why not me?
Wrong place, wrong time, maybe wrong family
Past Dreams fade away
Years disappear like smoke
The present an unfamiliar reality
How did I get here?
Twists & turns
Spinning through lets downs & disappointments
Apparently, I'm not who I thought I'd be
I look & see
Half
Sideshow mirror reflection
A vision distorted by dissection
& Half
Maybe this is exactly who I was meant to be
Been running so long
I lost sight of all the growth happening to me
Like a tree
Staring at the ground
Counting all the dead leaves
Keeping myself in winter

When it's really spring
What if all of this is God's timing?
I keep searching for a destination
When I know it's all about the journey
"Here" is a moment
Unlike any before
Unlike any after
A blessing
As delicate as a breath
As powerful as a dying star's last wish
We are star seeds manifested in flesh
A miracle of the highest order

So maybe I'm not who I thought I'd be
But perhaps
I'm more than I could have ever dreamed.

www.ingramcontent.com/pod-product-compliance
Lightning Source LLC
Chambersburg PA
CBHW051743130826
49812CB00033B/988
* 9 7 8 9 3 5 7 2 1 0 9 9 7 *